REALLY HORRIBLE JOKES

REALLY HORRIBLE BODY JOKES

KAREN KING

WINDMILL BOOKS

BOOKS

New York

Published in 2014 by Windmill Books, An Imprint of Rosen Publishing
29 East 21st Street, New York, NY 10010

First Edition

Editors: Patience Coster and Joe Harris
US Editor: Joshua Shadowens
All Images: Shutterstock
Layout Designer: Elaine Wilkinson
Cover Designers: Elaine Wilkinson and Trudi Webb

Library of Congress Cataloging-in-Publication Data

King, Karen, 1954 August 2–
 Really horrible body jokes / by Karen King.
    pages cm. — (Really horrible jokes)
 Includes index.
 ISBN 978-1-4777-9078-6 (library) — ISBN 978-1-4777-9079-3 (pbk.) —
ISBN 978-1-4777-9080-9
 1. Human body—Juvenile humor. I. Title.
 PN6231.H765K56 2014
 818'.602—dc23

                         2013021313

Printed in the USA
SL003841US

CPSIA Compliance Information: Batch #BW14WM: For Further Information contact Windmill Books, New York, New York at 1-866-478-0556

CONTENTS

GROSS BODY JOKES

What's the difference between boogers and broccoli?
Kids won't eat broccoli.

What has a bottom at the top?
Legs.

Did you hear the joke about the toilet?
I can't tell you, it's too dirty!

Did you hear about the man who lost the left side of his body?
He's all right now!

There was a young lady from Surrey
Who made a big pot of curry.
She ate the whole lot
Straight from the pot
And had to dash to the john in a hurry.

A belch is a gust of wind
That cometh from the heart,
But should it take a downward trend
It turneth to a fart.

Why did the man with one hand cross the road?
To get to the secondhand shop.

There was a young woman named Emma,
Who was seized with a terrible tremor.
She swallowed a spider,
Which wriggled inside her,
And left Emma in quite a dilemma.

What did one toilet say to the other?
You look flushed.

5

Knock, knock!
Who's there?
Tom Sawyer.
Tom Sawyer who?
Tom Sawyer butt when you were changing your underwear!

What do you do if your nose goes on strike?
Picket.

Why did the nose cross the road?
Because it was tired of getting picked on.

What did one eye say to the other?
Between you and me, something smells.

Laugh and the world laughs with you.
Fart and you stand alone.

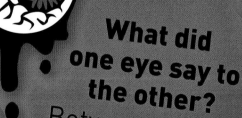

Why can't your nose be 12 inches long?
Because then it would be a foot!

Knock, knock!
Who's there?
Anita.
Anita who?
Anita go to the bathroom.

What do you call a woman with one leg shorter than the other?
Eileen.

What do you call someone who doesn't use a hankie?
Greensleeves.

What do you call someone who never blows his nose?
Ronnie.

There was an old man from Peru
Who dreamed he was eating his shoe.
He awoke in the night
In a terrible fright
And found it was perfectly true.

What do you call a man with a bus on his head?
Dead.

Which two letters are bad for your teeth?
D, K.

Knock, knock!
Who's there?
Dan.
Dan who?
Dandruff.

When are broken bones useful?
When they start to knit.

What do you always overlook? Your nose!

How do you keep a cold from going to your chest? Tie a knot in your neck.

When are eyes not eyes? When the wind makes them water.

What should you take if you're run down? The number of the car that hit you.

What goes "Ha, ha, bump?" A man laughing his head off.

HA, HA!

Why was the nose tired? Because it kept running.

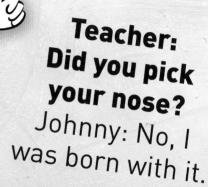

Teacher: Did you pick your nose? Johnny: No, I was born with it.

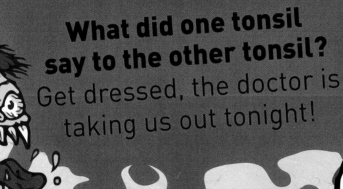

What did one tonsil say to the other tonsil? Get dressed, the doctor is taking us out tonight!

What color is a belch? Burple.

How many knees do people have? Four. Your left knee, your right knee, and your two kid-knees!

What is the perfect cure for dandruff?
Baldness.

Where do leeches keep their money?
At the blood bank.

Amy: My brother's in the hospital.
Ella: What's wrong with him?
Amy: He has spotted fever.
Ella: Is it dangerous?
Amy: No, it was spotted just in time.

What goes, "Boo, hoo, splat?"
Someone crying their eyes out.

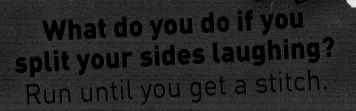

What do you do if you split your sides laughing?
Run until you get a stitch.

Did you hear the joke about the body snatchers?
I'd better not tell you, you might get carried away.

Why did the man put corn in his shoes?
Because he had pigeon toes.

Why did the secretary cut off her fingers?
She wanted to write shorthand.

Did you hear about the cross-eyed teacher?
He couldn't control his pupils.

There was a young man named Art
Who thought he'd be terribly smart.
He ate tons of beans
And busted his jeans
With a loud and earth-shattering fart.

Why did the farmer have sore feet?
A tractor ran over his corn.

How do you define agony?
A one-armed man with an itchy butt hanging from a clifftop.

What do you get if you feed a burglar cement?
A hardened criminal.

Doctor, I have a splitting headache.
Wait a minute while I find some glue.

GLUE

Why did the idiot burn his ear?
Someone called him while he was ironing.

Doctor, I've got a little stye.
Then you'd better buy a little pig.

Doctor, my nose keeps running, and I don't know what to do.
Stick your feet out in front, and trip it up.

Did you hear about the plastic surgeon who moved to a quiet, traditional village in the countryside? He certainly raised a few eyebrows!

Teacher: Where do you find germs? Pupil: In Germany!

What do you do if you swallow a spoon? Just sit there quietly and don't stir.

Doctor: I'm afraid you're overweight. Patient: I want a second opinion. **Doctor: Well, you're also rather ugly.**

Doctor, I'm having trouble getting to sleep. Lie on the edge of the bed and you'll soon drop off!

What happened when the idiot had a brain transplant? The brain rejected him.

What do you do if your kidneys are bad? Take them back to the butcher.

Doctor, my head is splitting. Let me ax you one or two questions.

Surgeon: I'm sorry, sir, but I left a sponge inside you when I operated last week. Patient: So that's why I keep feeling thirsty!

Doctor, I've got double vision. What can I do? Go around with one eye closed.

Doctor, will I be able to play the violin after my operation?
Yes, of course.
That's great news! I couldn't play it before...

Doctor, my hair keeps falling out. Can you give me something to keep it in?
Here's a box.

Doctor, help me, I swallowed a bone!
Are you choking?
No, I really did.

Doctor, I have stabbing pains in my gut.
And how long have you been a sword swallower?

Doctor, my son likes to pretend he's a small toilet.
Maybe he's a little potty.

17

Doctor, I've broken my arm in two places.
Well, don't go back there again!

Doctor: Why did you swallow a lightbulb?
Patient: Because everyone says I'm incredibly dim!

Did you hear about the plastic surgeon?
He sat in front of the fireplace and melted.

Doctor, can you give me something for wind?
Yes, here's a kite.

Doctor, I've got a terribly sore throat.
Go to the window and stick your tongue out.
Will that cure it?
No, I just don't like the woman who lives across the street.

Doctor, I keep getting a pain in my eye when I drink coffee.
Try taking the spoon out of the cup.

Doctor, I don't like all these flies buzzing around my head.
Point out the ones you do like, and I'll swat the rest.

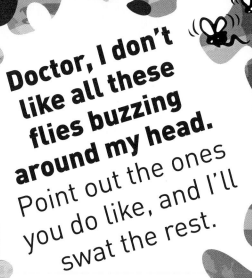

Doctor, I'm having trouble breathing.
I'll give you something that will soon put a stop to that!

Doctor, I'm so ugly, what can I do?
Advertise your services for Halloween parties.

Doctor, I keep thinking I'm a caterpillar. Don't worry, you'll soon change.

Jack: Have you seen the new doctor? He'll have you in stitches! Lily: I hope not. I've only come for a check-up!

Will this ointment clear my pimples, doctor? I never make rash promises.

What kind of bandage do people wear after heart surgery? Ticker tape.

A woman comes into the doctor's office with two little children who are crying. **"Why is your son crying?"** asks the doctor. "Because he has four peas stuck up his nose," explains the woman. **"And why is the little girl crying?"** "Because she wants the rest of her lunch back!"

Mother: Doctor, my son's just swallowed some gunpowder.
Doctor: Well, don't point him at me!

Surgeon to patient: I'm sorry to tell you that we've amputated the wrong leg. But don't worry, the man in the next bed wants to buy your shoes!

Patient: I'm really worried about my son's nail-biting habit.
Doctor: Don't worry, nail-biting is very common in children.
Patient: Even six-inch, rusty ones?

Worried patient: Tell me the truth, doctor, is it serious?
Doctor: Well, I wouldn't start watching any new TV series if I were you.

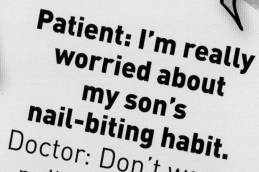
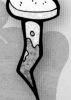

What do little zombies play?
Corpse and robbers.

What do you use to flatten a ghost?
A spirit level.

What did the zombie get his medal for?
Deadication.

Knock, knock!
Who's there?
Zombie.
Zombie who?
Zombies make honey, other bees are queens.

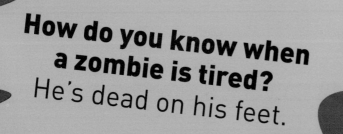

How do you know when a zombie is tired?
He's dead on his feet.

What do ghosts do on their vacations?
Fright-water rafting.

What rooms don't zombies like?
Living rooms.

What streets do ghosts haunt?
Dead ends.

What do you call a brainy monster?
Frank Einstein.

Why was the vampire lurking in the shadows? He was waiting for his necks victim.

What do ghosts like to play at a party? Hide and shriek.

What do ghosts eat for dessert? Boo-berry pie!

Who did the ghost invite to his party? Anyone he could dig up.

Why didn't the skeleton play music in church?
Because he had no organs.

Why do vampires like giraffes?
...e they ...h long ...ks.

...d has sharp teeth?
...olding his breath.

What do you get if you cross an ice cube with a vampire?
Frostbite.

ARKANSAS TEEN BOOK AWARD

2021-2022
Level 1

Clap When You Land
by Elizabeth Acevedo

The Inheritance Games
by Jennifer Lynn Barnes

Stamped: Racism, Antiracism, and You
by Jason Reynolds, Ibram X. Kendi

Legendborn
by Tracy Deonn

When Stars Are Scattered
by Victoria Jamieson, Omar Mohamed
Illustrated by Iman Geddy

...s a ...pire's ...ite fruit?
...neck-tarine.

25

Why do vampires drink blood? Because coffee makes them jittery.

What did the zombie's friend say when he saw his new girlfriend? Good grief! Where did you dig her up from?

First ghoul: Am I late for dinner? Second ghoul: Yes, everyone's been eaten.

Who looks after a haunted house? Skeleton staff.

Knock, knock! Who's there? **Turner** Turner who? **Turner round very slowly, there's a zombie behind you!**

Where do you go to buy a zombie? To the mon-store.

Why do ghosts like strawberries for dessert? Because they come with scream.

Knock Knock
Who's there?
The interrupting ghost.
The interrupting gho—
Wooooooo!

Where do zombies go on cruises? The Dead-iterranean Sea.

What does Dracula say to his victims?
It's been nice gnawing you.

Why is Hollywood full of vampires?
They need someone to play the bit parts.

What do you call an overweight vampire?
Draculard.

What do vampires play poker for?
High stakes.

How do you catch a vampire fish?
With bloodworms.

Did you hear about the nervous vampire?
He kept fainting at the sight of blood!

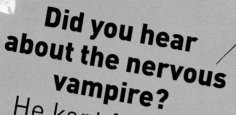

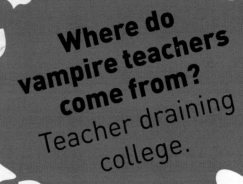

Where do vampire teachers come from?
Teacher draining college.

What is the best pet for a vampire?
A bloodhound.

What is a vampire's favorite sport?
Bat-minton!

How does Dracula like to have his food served?
In bite-sized pieces.

How can you tell if a vampire is sick?
He keeps coffin!

What is a cannibal's favorite party game?
Swallow my leader.

Why was the vampire locked up in an asylum?
He was completely batty.

Why is drinking blood a complete waste of time?
It is all in vein.

What is the U.S. national holiday for vampires?
Fangs-giving Day.

What did the cannibal chef make of his new kitchen assistant?
Burgers!

Why was the cannibal expelled from school?
Because he kept buttering up the teachers.

Why are vampires so annoying?
They are all pains in the neck.

Why do vampires never get fat?
They eat necks to nothing.

Glossary

Further Reading

Borgenicht, David. *Monkeyfarts!: Wacky Jokes Every Kid Should Know.* Philadelphia, PA: Quirk Books, 2012.

Hawkins, Jay. *Really Horrible Body Facts.* Really Horrible Facts. New York: Windmill Books, 2014.

Weintraub, Aileen. *The Everything Kids' Gross Jokes Book.* Avon, MA: Adams Media, 2005.

Websites

For web resources related to the subject of this book, go to: www.windmillbooks.com/weblinks and select this book's title.

Index